CHAMPION SPORT

BIOGRAPHIES

RONALDO

CHAMPION SPORT

BIOGRAPHIES

RONALDO

MARK PADDOCK

W

Warwick Publishing Inc.

Toronto   Los Angeles

www.warwickgp.com

We acknowledge the financial support of the Government of Canada through the Book Publishing Industry Development Program for our publishing activities.

ISBN: 1-894020-60-X

Published by Warwick Publishing Inc.
162 John Street, Suite 300, Toronto, Ontario, Canada M5V 2E5

Cover and layout design: Heidi Gemmill
Editorial Services: Joseph Romain

Printed and bound in Canada

Cover and interior photos courtesy AP/Wide World Photos

To Jennifer who, like Ronaldo, is uniquely inspiring

Table of Contents

Factsheet

Ronaldo Luis Nazario de Lima

Birth Date: September 18, 1976

Place of Birth: Bento Ribeiro, Brazil

Height: 6 feet 1 inch (183 centimetres)

Weight: 180 pounds (82 kilograms)

Career Highlights:

1994 - reserve player on Brazil's team for the World Cup
- Mineiro championship scoring leader
- Super Cup scoring leader

1995 - Dutch championship scoring leader

1996 - Dutch Cup (with Eindhoven)
- Olympic bronze medal with Brazilian national soccer team
- FIFA World Player of the Year

1997 - Spanish league scoring leader
- Latin American Player of the Year, Spanish league
- Cup-Winners Cup (with FC Barcelona)
- European Player of the Year
- Copa America
- FIFA/Confederations Cup
- FIFA World Player of the Year

1998 - UEFA Cup (with Inter Milan)
- Italian league Player of the Year
- European Forward of the Year
- European Player of the Year
- World Cup Golden Ball (Best Player)

Introduction

On June 10, 1998, more than 80,000 excited fans swarmed into the Stade de France to watch Brazil, the mighty champions, play Scotland. It was the opening match of the World Cup, the world championship for the game of football (or soccer, as it is known in North America).

The sun glinted on the golden sweater of Brazil's number 9, Ronaldo, as he strode down the right side of the field and gathered a pass from teammate Cafu. Sensing that Scotland captain Colin Hendry was closing in from behind, Ronaldo paused. As Hendry reached him, Ronaldo spun around to face his pursuer. Hendry stopped, his eyes wide and surprised. Ronaldo immediately ran sideways, losing Hendry and another defender. He fooled yet another Scot with a quick flick of his hips, then broke free to shoot at the goalie.

Journalists were stunned at this piece of imagination. How many players would think to run backwards, then sideways, to escape a tackle? How many could actually do it? It defied all the usual practices of soccer.

While many players wear number 9 for their national teams, there is only one Ronaldo. He is the greatest soccer player of this era. His mother, Sonia, might even say he was destined to be the best. Before he was born, a witch doctor—a powerful disciple of magic—had visited Sonia. He had looked into the future and made a prediction:

"A boy will come and illuminate your life and make you a millionaire."

When her third child turned out to be a boy, she named him Ronaldo and took special care of him. With her guidance, Ronaldo found the strength to succeed. The results have been seen all around the world, in soccer stadiums and on televisions.

No one really knows how greatness happens, but in Ronaldo's case, it seemed that fate chose a unique role for him.

Chapter 1

The Early Years

In the dirty streets of Bento Ribeiro, Brazil, where life was desperate and dangerous, a small boy with big teeth chased a plastic ball with his friends. He was just one of many poor children who had nothing else to do as they grew up in the *favelas*, or slums, during the 1980s.

The boy was a good player, but no one except his peers seemed to notice it. And none of them could have predicted the future of their friend, Ronaldo Luis Nazario de Lima, as a witch doctor had done. Looking back years later, his friend Marcio Perez stated, "No one ever thought he would be the best in the world." But that's exactly what happened.

Ronaldo came into the world on September 18, 1976, in a crowded and run-down hospital room that echoed with the cries of newborn babies and mothers in labor. His father, Nelio, was nowhere in sight. Sonia, his mother, was not surprised, for her husband was in love with the dangerous chemical high of alcohol. When Ronaldo was born, his father might have been in the middle of a day-long drinking spell, or he might have been lost in the dark magic of drugs, another weakness. These were expensive habits, especially for a man who held a low-paying job at a telephone company.

When Nelio learned that his son had been born in the Sao Francisco Javier Medical Centre, he didn't have the money to pay for Ronaldo's birth registration. This act was necessary so that the government would have an official record of Ronaldo's existence. It took Nelio four days to find the money, the equivalent of 10 American dollars. When he finally registered his son, he pretended the birth had happened that very day, September 22. For many years, only his family knew Ronaldo's true birthday.

Sonia brought Ronaldo home to General Cesar Obino Street, introducing her son Nelio Jr., or Nelinho, and her daughter Ione to their new brother. There was little space for three children in the house: it consisted of a single bedroom, a kitchen and a living room stuffed underneath a low roof. Once Ronaldo turned five, he had to sleep on the living room couch with Nelinho. The family had no telephone and no fridge. A television set was their only luxury.

When Ronaldo was old enough to walk, he discovered he wasn't living in a beautiful place. Next to his tiny house stood two more shacks, occupied by Ronaldo's aunts, uncles and cousins. Beyond, the narrow street was dusty and full of wrecked cars. Many of the nearby houses lacked windows and doors. And everything was lopsided, because Bento Ribeiro lay on the side of a hill, just north of Rio de Janeiro, the former capital city of Brazil. Rio is hilly, especially in the north, but Ronaldo's favela lacked water pipes or sewers, so it had to be on a mountain; that way, waste could drain away naturally.

The seaport of Rio is set in southeast Brazil, 1,600 miles (2,500 km) below the equator, within fertile farm country. Outside the city, fields full of bright oranges stretch for miles. Much of Rio is just as attractive: its long, white beaches, which include the world-famous Copacabana, are flanked by delicate palm trees. Its south section houses a botanical garden, full of rare tropical plants, and a lake.

There are rich neighborhoods with well-designed apartment blocks and expensive hotels. From his hill-side, Ronaldo could see some of this, but it might as well have been on the moon. Without money, he could not escape the favela.

Escape was the one idea in everyone's mind, but there were different ways to do it. The older children and teenagers commonly used drugs and alcohol. When they were drunk or drugged, they could forget about their sad lives. They knew they lived in a country where poor people were not cared for by the rest of society. In fact, many politicians and businessmen thought the poor were an embarrassment. The most corrupt authorities would bribe policemen to kill poor children who wandered the streets. Ronaldo and his friends never were sure when it was safe to be outside.

Like their younger neighbors, many adults became drug addicts and alcoholics. Others watched television constantly. After Ronaldo was born, Sonia found a job working long hours in a small restaurant, but when she came home, she would watch soap operas. They were badly written fantasies in which beautiful women and handsome men experienced an endless series of great and terrible events. The soap operas were poor art, but at least they didn't destroy your body and mind like drugs.

For those who were athletic, soccer was the escape. When Ronaldo turned four, his father gave him a plastic ball as a Christmas present. It was Ronaldo's first important possession, apart from a teddy bear. He found an empty piece of land on the edge of town, and he and his friends began to play soccer there regularly.

Because he was so young, the others rarely passed Ronaldo the ball. He had to learn to take it by force. He also had to cope with unpredictable bounces on the rocky, uneven earth, and the cuts and bruises he received on his bare feet and legs. But he was determined, and he ran around the rough pitch wildly, without stopping. He played throughout the warm winter and the cooler summer, and within a year, he was one of the best players in the favela.

Ronaldo quickly became obsessed with the game of soccer. When he was asleep, dreaming, he would yell at his teammates to pass him the ball. He would even try to kick it. Once he started school, lessons didn't interest him. He had found his subject already, and it couldn't be learned in the classroom.

"I felt that soccer was my natural profession, my role in life," he said later.

Often, he and his friends would play soccer in the streets, barefoot, when they should have been in school. His mother thought this was a terrible mistake. A hard-working lady with strong moral standards, Sonia believed education was the key to improving Ronaldo's life. She knew sports didn't guarantee a good future. Her brother, Pipico, had played professional soccer, but he was no richer than Sonia and Nelio. Sonia would take Ronaldo to school and wait outside for up to an hour to make sure he didn't leave. Ronaldo reacted by quitting his classes when she was gone.

While Ronaldo was committed and focused as a footballer, he was a very different person off the field. As a baby and a small boy, his parents noticed that he would cry if he was put to sleep in the dark. They had to leave a light on. Later, he began to walk in his sleep, and this increased his fear of darkness. If he came home after sunset, he would refuse to enter the house unless a light was shining.

Ronaldo also seemed to be timid around most people. He often cried. He did not speak much, and when he did, his large, badly formed teeth made his words unclear.

In the streets, Nelinho had to make sure no one bullied his younger brother. At home, Ronaldo was much more energetic and playful. His mother Sonia and sister Ione, who was four years older, protected and coddled him, making him feel safe and confident when they were present.

Apart from his family, only soccer gave Ronaldo the same security he felt at home. His cousin Fabio Shine observed that "when he was playing football, he seemed to change character and become a real man." Fabio also thought the only way Ronaldo could express himself was through soccer.

Unlike Sonia, Ronaldo's father Nelio was a parent who understood his son's fascination with "the beautiful game," as soccer fans call their favorite sport. A dedicated player himself, Nelio claimed that several Brazilian pro teams had asked him to join them.

Nelio took Ronaldo to see his first pro match at Rio's Maracana Stadium, the biggest soccer house in the world. Almost 200,000 fans could squeeze into the ugly, decaying building that was built to host the 1950 World Cup.

Like many others, Ronaldo beat a drum to encourage the home team, Flamengo. He and his father joined the cries of "Flamengo, Flamengo" that echoed from thousands around them. Depending on what happened on the pitch, the fans were angry, disappointed, joyful, amazed—they were deeply involved in every play. And no matter what happened, they were loud.

Ronaldo never had experienced such passion, and he would remember it for the rest of his life. He had discovered his countrymen were crazy about soccer.

When he was nine, in the winter of 1986 (in the southern hemisphere, winter comes in June and July), Ronaldo joined a boys' team called Valqueire. But he was late for the first tryout, so he had to agree to become a goaltender, the least popular position for any Brazilian. Goalies couldn't score or make breathtaking plays, like all the great Brazilian players seemed to do.

Luckily, Ronaldo had to switch to forward when injuries hit the team. By the time he was 10, he had well-developed leg muscles and a strong body: a sign of things to come.

Alirio Jose de Carvalho, who coached an 11-year-old Ronaldo at Social Ramos, saw that he was different: Ronaldo had no fear, and he never seemed to be upset by his opponents. Ronaldo netted 166 goals that season, including 11 in one game. Once again, he showed that on the field, he became a stronger, more confident person.

Maybe he had to be, for that was a bad year for Ronaldo at home. His parents Nelio and Sonia had been apart for long periods, but now they finally decided to divorce. Ronaldo was shocked and angry, but at least he could work out his feelings by kicking a soccer.

Ronaldo also refined his skill on the Copacabana Beach. Bento Ribeiro was a railway town, built only to service the railroad that was constructed late in the 1700s. Ronaldo would take the train from Bento to Rio with his friends, hiding to avoid paying a fare he did not have. Then he would join the huge crowds that stretched for miles along the beach. As far as he could see, there were small groups with soccer balls, each playing their own game.

Sometimes Ronaldo played in the usual way, and other times he would find a volleyball net and kick the ball back and forth over it. Since the tiny grains of sand on the beach were slippery and shifty, he had to learn balance and strong passing and trapping skills. Ronaldo played barefoot, another factor that encouraged skilled play, for with each mis-kick he would hurt his feet.

By the age of 13, the young striker's reputation had become so good that Flamengo asked him to attend a tryout. Flamengo had developed a great, attacking style that lifted it to the top of the most-popular list in Brazil.

Ronaldo would have been the perfect player for the team he already loved, but he never had a chance to put on its famous jersey. He was so poor that, at the tryout, he asked the team to pay his bus fare to and from the stadium if he was accepted. Flamengo wanted him, but it refused his request. Already upset by the team's refusal, Ronaldo was robbed of his watch by two boys on his way home. Sonia remembered that when he got back, he "cried and cried."

HIs failure to make the team cut him deeply, and Ronaldo thought about quitting soccer. But his obsession with the game remained. Already, he had told people that he wanted to be the best, become rich and help his family out of poverty.

Ronaldo was rescued by Coach de Carvalho at Social Ramos. De Carvalho suggested that Sao Cristovao should give him a chance. The Rio-based club, which played in Brazil's Second Division, accepted him. He lived nearby, so travel was not a problem.

Ronaldo's first experience of professional soccer gave him a taste of what hard work on the pitch could bring him and his family. After playing for them for a while, the team gave his family a house near its field. It was a typical, working-class residence, but it had running water and sewage lines. To Ronaldo and his sister and brother, it was far better than the house they had grown up in. At last, they had left the depressing favela behind.

In the end, Ronaldo quit school, not soccer; he left in his seventh year. There were no more distractions; sports now occupied his entire life.

Ronaldo's new coach, Alfredo Sampaio, thought he looked "wooden" at first, but over the next two seasons, Ronaldo scored 36 goals in 54 games. Many top professionals would have been thrilled with these numbers.

Sampaio began to notice the same qualities in his striker that the world would see eventually. A natural athlete, Ronaldo had no interest in tactics and strategy. He only wanted to score in the most spectacular way he could. He had discovered that goals gave him more pleasure than anything else. If he was asked to play defensively, Ronaldo would refuse. He didn't even seem interested in the game if someone else had the ball.

Ronaldo's closest friend on the Sao Cristovao team was Calango, whom he had known from childhood. One day, after a soccer practice on Copacabana Beach, the two friends decided to swim out to sea on borrowed surfboards.

The waves were swelling up to 12 feet (3.5 m) high, and the ocean looked threatening, but the young and foolish friends did not turn back. Calango looked up and saw a gigantic wave, bigger than the rest, sweeping down upon them. He screamed at Ronaldo, telling him to stay low.

Then the wall of blue water collapsed on them. They plummeted into the depths like falling anchors, unable to breathe, held underwater by the intense pressure of the wave. Ronaldo's leg smashed into Calango.

"I'm going to die!" Calango thought in despair.

Ronaldo was thrown right into his friend, and the two grabbed each other. Together, they flew into the air and landed on the beach. Somehow, they had survived. They agreed it was a miracle from God.

Fortune continued to smile upon Ronaldo, just as the witch doctor had predicted to his mother years before. The turning point of his career came when Jairzinho spotted him at a San Cristovao match. Jairzinho had been a great soccer player, a member of the 1970 Brazilian team that Pele led to the World Cup championship. This was a man who could recognize soccer talent.

Jairzinho told two agents they should consider signing Ronaldo. As agents, Reinaldo Pitta and Alexandre Martins were in charge of business deals for any players who hired them under a legal contract. They asked Ronaldo's father, Nelio, if he would consider signing his son to a contract with them.

Nelio had spent a couple of years away from

Ronaldo after the divorce, but he had reappeared when he heard how talented his son was. He supported Ronaldo's soccer career, and he agreed to sign his son to a 10-year contract with Pitta and Martins. In 1993, the two arranged a transfer for Ronaldo. He would join Cruzeiro of the First Division.

At age 17, Ronaldo had made it to the top level of national soccer. Within a year, he would be a star.

Chapter 2

Growing Up and Growing Famous

In January 1998, Ronaldo was the star of a live chat on the Internet, the world-wide computer network. For the second year in a row, he was helping the United Nations' Food and Agriculture Organization fight against hunger.

But his question-and-answer session had to be cut off after half an hour when over six million people tried to join it. The computer system could not handle the hailstorm of inquiries, and it broke down. No other footballer would have commanded so much attention.

It was an amazing accomplishment for a 21-year-old, especially one who had been born with few advantages. But Ronaldo had committed every bit of himself to soccer at an early age. He had become great in a very short time, partly because he had a unique talent, and partly because he had endless determination. However, he was now so famous that fame, not soccer, threatened to become the most dominant part of his life.

The young striker first thrilled fans in his home country of Brazil as a member of Cruzeiro, in Belo Horizonte, when he scored 58 goals in a 60-game season. In his best game, he made the opposing goalie look silly by scoring five times. Stocky, with tremendous leg muscles, Ronaldo had the ability to race past or even right through defenders.

Playing in large stadiums, with many thousands cheering on, he was inspired, not intimidated. He discovered he loved an audience. Brazilians immediately saw him as their next soccer hero, and they named him "Ronaldinho," or Little Ronaldo. From then on, no one bothered to call him by his full name.

This was not unusual: almost every Brazilian player was known by a nickname. But it was a sign that Ronaldo had arrived for good. The media began to write and talk about him seven days a week.

The Brazilian national team quickly took advantage of Ronaldo's exploding talent. In March 1994, coach Carlos Parreira played him as a substitute against Argentina. In his next international match against Iceland, he scored. He was so impressive that he made the Brazilian national team for World Cup 94, but the coaches decided he would face too much pressure if he played. Ronaldo watched from the sidelines as Romario led Brazil to its fourth championship.

Even without stepping on the field, Ronaldo was praised. When Canadian journalists asked some

Brazilian reporters about the best players on their team, they complimented Romario and Bebeto, the two dangerous strikers, but said, "Wait until you see Ronaldo."

Coach Parreira was wise to let Ronaldo watch rather than play at that point. Despite all of his fine qualities, he was only 17. Some children mature rapidly if they have a difficult life, but this hadn't happened to Ronaldo. He was still shy and uncertain, and one reporter claimed that "you could see the tears of fear welling up in his eyes" as he sat on the Brazilian bench. How would he have coped as billions watched him play?

There were other signs of immaturity too. When reporters came to him, Ronaldo had trouble voicing his thoughts. Whenever he saw a pretty girl, he would stare and stare, not realizing how rude it was. Only the journalists realized it.

Part of Ronaldo's insecurity came from his looks. His teeth were still too big and stuck out too much, while his short, curly hair always seemed to grow unevenly. Pitta and Martins, his agents, decided he had to improve his appearance. If he looked good, he would be easier to promote to the public and to advertisers. They asked him to shave his head, and they bought him braces for his teeth.

The bald look suited Ronaldo, and the braces eventually straightened out his teeth a lot. When they were taken off several months later, he looked like a different person. He had an unexpressive face to begin with, for his emotions usually stayed hidden, but now it seemed older and tougher. If he flashed his warm yet shy smile, the effect was diminished, and the old Ronaldo returned for a moment.

With his image remade, Ronaldo transferred to PSV Eindhoven in the Netherlands after one season with Cruzeiro. PSV paid 6 million dollars for the right to have him. (The team selling a player receives most of the money in a transfer, while the player and his agents usually receive from 5 to 10 per cent.) Never before had a teenager commanded such a high transfer fee.

Besides the money, it was a good move in other ways as well. The best leagues were located in Europe, and almost every great South American found his way there sooner or later. While the Dutch league was strong, it was not as challenging as those in Spain, England or Italy. It was an good place to start for a young player.

Immediately, the fan mail began to rain down on Eindhoven. Long before his first Dutch season was over, Ronaldo had answered more than 2,000 letters with a letter of his own and a signed picture. One-third of these were sent to Brazilian fans.

Ronaldo's favorite musicians were a group of Brazilians known as Gabriel O Pensador, and when they heard this, they invited him to appear in a music video. In the video, the group drove around Rio on a bus, and Ronaldo pretended to be the bus conductor. The video showed how Ronaldo's existence had changed, for it was a dark but amusing commentary on the sadness and pain of life in Rio: the place where drugs were sold openly, where people were shot down in the streets. In the old days, the song could have applied to Ronaldo's life. Now he was beyond it, but there were new challenges ahead.

One of these was homesickness. Ronaldo had left his warm South American home for a cooler, northern European country. The flat countryside of the Netherlands, with its open farmlands, looked a bit similar to the plateaus of southern Brazil, where he had lived.

But the culture was very different from the Latin society Ronaldo was used to. The Netherlands was a tiny country and very densely populated. As a result, the Dutch, while pleasant, were more dedicated to social rules and regulations. They needed order and self-discipline if they were to co-exist in a small space. They were definitely not like Brazilians, who showed their feelings without shame and often exaggerated them.

Ronaldo felt out of place, so much so that he usually stayed at home in between matches. He was suffering from culture shock: that sense of confusion you feel when moving to a foreign place you don't understand.

He was only 18. He had never seen Europe before and suddenly he was living there without his family. He didn't like the Dutch food, and he dreamed about his mother's cooking. He wouldn't drive the car that his team had given him. He spent many hours doing nothing more than watching films and soccer on television.

Then, one day, he burst into tears as he spoke to his mother on the phone. Always protective—often overly protective—of her son, Sonia decided she had to help him, so she flew to Eindhoven to stay for a while. She didn't return home to Rio until eight months later.

Since childhood, Ronaldo had enjoyed a special bond with his mother. Like many Latin mothers, Sonia thrust herself into every part of her son's life, making sure he always knew what she thought. He had been timid and unsure as a boy, so it was easy for her to be involved; Ronaldo needed and wanted her guidance. Once his father Nelio left the family, the bond between mother and son deepened in Ronaldo's crucial teenage years.

Ronaldo hid nothing from his mother, and he was at his most natural around her. In Eindhoven, he loved to entertain Sonia: he would ride his bike through the house, yelling and singing, or wrestle her to the floor. If she was nearby, Ronaldo was happy.

Ronaldo found someone else to help him: a girl-friend, Nadia, who came from Rio. This marked the third time he had enjoyed a romance, but each time, his mother seemed to complicate matters. In Belo Horizonte, he had met a nice girl called Luciana, and they dated for six months. But when Sonia felt Luciana wasn't good enough for her son, Ronaldo broke up with her.

Ronaldo's second romance was with a pretty girl called Katia. When Katia told the Brazilian public who her boyfriend was during World Cup 94, Sonia decided this was unacceptable. She refused to let Katia speak to Ronaldo any more.

In Eindhoven, Nadia lived with Ronaldo and his mother, but Sonia made it clear that Nadia wasn't the right match for her special son. Sonia only had good intentions: she wanted someone who would place Ronaldo's career first and support him at every turn. Nadia didn't appear to do so. Ronaldo trusted his mother's insight, but he trusted it too much—he lacked strength and independence. When Sonia made sly comments that criticized Nadia, Ronaldo was silent.

When his first season in the Netherlands ended, Ronaldo had captured the league's goal-scoring title, and it was clear he had adjusted to the higher skill level of Dutch soccer. PSV did well too, placing second in the standings.

Off the field, there were also positive signs. Ronaldo's new appearance gave him some confidence. He was more outgoing, more ready to laugh, and he even showed that he could disagree with his mother.

When she told a houseguest that "Ronaldo is on earth to score," he criticized her openly. It seemed as if his culture shock and his old insecurities were fading.

After an injury-shortened second season with PSV, FC Barcelona in Spain paid a $20-million transfer fee for Ronaldo in 1996. Barcelona was a great team that played in a country full of passionate Latin fans and journalists. Ronaldo had been appreciated in the Netherlands, but he had not been adored.

Furthermore, the media spotlight wasn't very bright there, and he had played without getting much attention. In some ways, going to Spain was like playing in Brazil again. The whole country would hear about what he did each day.

In Barcelona, a large port city in northern Spain with over one million residents, Ronaldo could go to the sandy beaches, play a casual game of soccer, or swim, just as he had done in Rio. Naturally, he decided to live by the Mediterranean Sea in Castelldefels, a suburb. In an environment that was far more familiar and comfortable than Eindhoven, Ronaldo was sure to be happier.

Barcelona was an interesting city as well. People had lived there for more than two thousand years. For at least half that time, the city had been a center of commerce, exporting goods across the Mediterranean Sea in ships. Now, ancient, elegant churches and towers sat side by side with gleaming, modern factories, office buildings and hotels. FC Barcelona played in the magnificent Camp Nou stadium, a skyscraper that dominated the streets around it. The stadium symbolized the love and honor that Spaniards had for the beautiful game.

The Spanish fans liked Ronaldo immediately. They called him "Little Buddha"—with his shaved head and wide, serious face, he resembled pictures of the Buddha, the man who had founded the Buddhist faith centuries ago. Like the Buddha, Ronaldo had inspired a group of devoted followers, but not every religious leader was happy about it. One Catholic bishop in Barcelona complained that paintings of the Last Supper, a major event in the Bible, had been removed from public places and replaced by posters of Ronaldo.

Now 19, Ronaldo continued the fabulous scoring pace he had established in Cruzeiro and PSV: almost one goal a game. Playing with top footballers who could feed him precise passes, he looked unstoppable at times. Adoring journalists called him a genius. They said he belonged in the same class as Pele and Maradona, the legendary South Americans who had come before him.

Even the opposing fans liked Ronaldo. When FC Barcelona flew to Madrid in December 1996 to play Real, their hated rivals, about 2,000 locals cheered him as he entered the airport. It was an amazing, almost unbelievable sight. A crowd of 106,000 people filled Real's stadium to gasp at his moves, and 500 journalists studied the event first-hand. Suddenly, Ronaldo was becoming a superstar.

Whenever possible, reporters surrounded Ronaldo, asking him endless questions about his health, his personal life, his opponents and anything else they wanted to know. Hot, bright camera lights shone into his eyes, making him blink. Microphones and tape recorders pressed into his face. It was as if the journalists were hunters and he was their prey.

But Ronaldo had developed the strength to deal with them. He would answer courteously, patiently, speaking more freely and intelligently than he had done in Brazil or the Netherlands. As the media's demands on him grew, he grew with them. But when he had reached his limit, he might slip away in the middle of a question. He was still a private man.

Once, Ronaldo showed the public a flash of the lightheartedness that generally only surfaced at home. Attending the opening of a Barcelona restaurant, he was asked to pose for photographs with famous model Cindy Crawford. He jokingly replied that Cindy should have been asked to pose with him instead. Another time, on the team airplane, he walked into the cockpit, turned on the public address system and recited a list of his coach's favorite sayings in a mocking voice.

Not many knew about his childlike side either. When his sister Ione visited him in Europe with her baby, she commented that Ronaldo made sure he was the first to play with her son's new toys. Ronaldo's favorite toy was the teddy bear. It was one of the few things that had comforted him in childhood, so it carried good memories. He even collected toy bears.

Childhood was a long way in the past, though. The world of adult games, where a fortune could be made by kicking a ball, was the place Ronaldo now inhabited. Agents Pitta and Martins had foreseen his popularity. When Ronaldo signed his contract with Barcelona, they made sure the club paid him an additional $8 million for the right to sell shirts, medals and other souvenirs bearing his name. Only the best and most loved players had the power to create this kind of deal, and Ronaldo was now one of them.

Chapter 3

Soccer Superstar

In his short time abroad, Ronaldo had moved to a level of fame reached by very few athletes, one where his name and face were recognized even by those who were not devoted fans of his sport.

As his success in Europe skyrocketed, Ronaldo's fame in his native Brazil increased even more. In Rio, drivers and pedestrians often saw his face smiling at them from huge billboard ads. It seemed that every company wanted Ronaldo to promote a product.

Since he appeared to be able to score whenever he pleased, he had acquired a magical aura. One restaurant owner in Barcelona was so convinced of the striker's charisma that he paid him $160,000 simply to appear in the building for a short time. FC Barcelona had targeted the food market already by creating a "Ronaldoburger" at a restaurant in its stadium.

At the start of 1997, Ronaldo signed the biggest marketing contract of his career with Nike, the giant international sporting goods company. Nike only chose the brightest stars to represent its products: Pete

Sampras in tennis, golfer Tiger Woods, car racer Michael Schumacher, and, of course, Michael Jordan.

Nike would pay Ronaldo about $2 million a year for 10 years. The firm named a line of clothes after Ronaldo and invented a new soccer shoe, the Mercurial, especially for him. In return, he was expected to appear in Nike ads and make public appearances on behalf of the company. With Nike's expertise and financial power behind him, Ronaldo's name and face would be sent into every corner of the world.

Ronaldo celebrated the deal by winning the FIFA World Player of the Year award for 1996. He received 54 first-place votes, far ahead of Liberia's George Weah, who had 16, and England's Alan Shearer, who had 11. His rocket, which had climbed so rapidly, had reached the top after only four years of First Division soccer.

Ronaldo had more to think about than awards, though. Late in 1996, his personal life had taken a dramatic turn. His relationship with Nadia had not survived, and he was dating another Brazilian, Adeli. But in the summer of 1996, after winning a bronze medal with the Brazilian team at the Atlanta Olympics, Ronaldo had spent an evening in a Rio bar. He almost never drank alcohol—he had seen how it ruined his father—but he liked to dance, and he was more outgoing than before. In Belo Horizonte, the female fans had begun to follow him, and his recent romances gave him the confidence to approach them.

On the dance floor, Ronaldo saw a beautiful, slim blonde. He could not pull his eyes away, for she had a look that was considered ideal in Rio. They danced together and had a long conversation. She had a cute, almost innocent way of seeing things. He found out that she was Suzanna Werner, a model who wanted to become a famous actress. Ronaldo thought she was enchanting, but she refused to let him phone her afterwards. She would not reveal her telephone number. The reason was simple. Suzanna already had a boyfriend, and he was the jealous type.

Still unable to forget the girl with the bubbly personality, Ronaldo received some stunning news from a friend several months later: Suzanna's boyfriend had died in a motorcycle crash. Ronaldo's friend uncovered Suzanna's number, and Ronaldo made the phone call he had wanted to make for so long.

But Suzanna didn't believe it was him, and she kept hanging up. Finally, he described how they had met, and she realized it was truly him. After several weeks of constant calls, Ronaldo admitted that he had been in love with her since they met.

Suzanna had been attracted to the young footballer as well. With his little-boy smile and quiet, humble manner, Ronaldo hardly acted like a star. Once their feelings were out in the open, they had to meet. Ronaldo flew into Rio. After dark, Suzanna drove to a prearranged meeting spot in Leblon, a suburban area. Then she hid in the back seat, and Ronaldo arrived to drive them away. They were very careful because they didn't want the media to see or photograph them together. When Ronaldo stopped the car, he kissed her for the first time. Suzanna would always remember it as a wonderful moment.

The fact that Ronaldo lived in Castelldefels, Spain, while Suzanna lived across the Atlantic in Barra de Tijuca, a rich Rio suburb, did not stop either of them from dating. In fact, Ronaldo was so absorbed by Suzanna that he flew back to Rio four times between early December and mid-January to visit her. It cost him $15,000, but he didn't even notice.

Just when Ronaldo seemed ready to adjust to life in Europe, he had found the most powerful reason of all to go home. He also discovered that love has a way of disrupting your job. He was a professional athlete, obligated to follow a tight schedule of matches and practices. His manager, Bobby Robson, and his teammates all expected him to be devoted to the team. But for the moment, it was clear that Suzanna came first and everything else came second.

After one late-December trip to Rio, Ronaldo stumbled out of the Barcelona airport. He was so tired from the long flight that he couldn't find his car. He ran around the parking lot until he located his expensive BMW, then raced to a training session at Camp Nou. He was two days late. Robson punished him with a New Year's Day detention, but Ronaldo still managed to fly home for New Year's Eve and return early the next day.

As well as breaking team rules, Ronaldo's jetsetting was hurting his fitness. The long, cross-Atlantic flights gave him jet lag, and a tired footballer could not always be a great one. Still, he managed to score a goal in almost every game he played. Ronaldo's style, which combines sudden bursts with long, quiet spells, helped him, but it seemed he simply had the ability to perform under any circumstance. Like Maradona and the other superstars, he could leave his personal life behind when he ran on the field.

Even so, Ronaldo's actions were not forgiven or forgotten by some of his teammates. A few already felt envious of his fame and his salary—at least $1.5 million per season—and they didn't understand why he stayed away from them so much. When he missed such things as a retirement dinner for team captain Jose Mari Bakero, people whispered about it.

But as a basically shy man, Ronaldo didn't like to be in crowds, among those whom he couldn't trust. No matter how much time he spent in Barcelona, he would have avoided these social events.

There is almost always friction within a professional sports team, and if the club is good enough, it rises above the problem. FC Barcelona did that, running to the final of the Cup-Winners Cup, one of three trophies available to the top European clubs. Most clubs could compete only inside their national leagues, but the best ones qualified to play against teams from other European countries for the Cup-Winners Cup, the UEFA Cup and the Champions Cup.

The boys from Barcelona faced a challenging foe in the final—Paris St-Germain (PSG) from France. PSG was the defending champion. Like Barcelona, it had a Brazilian connection: Rai and Leonardo, both crucial players. Midfielder Rai knew what he was up against.

"Ronaldo doesn't doubt himself, he's very natural," Rai stated.

To make matters worse, the marvelously gifted Hristo Stoichkov teamed with Little Buddha to form a lethal forward duo. PSG had its hands full.

Forty-five-thousand excited fans, many from Paris and Barcelona, filled the stadium in Rotterdam, the Netherlands, to watch the clash. As he ran onto the field, Ronaldo made the sign of the Roman Catholic cross, as he always did, praying for good fortune.

The first half was tough, grinding soccer, not the kind that suited Ronaldo's attacking style. But then, in the 37th minute, he accepted a pass and charged into the penalty area. A panicky defender tripped him, forcing the referee to call a penalty shot.

Ronaldo placed the ball on the 12-yard marker. The PSG players retreated, clearing the box. Ronaldo was alone against the goalie, Bernard Lama. He stepped back several paces.

The referee blew his whistle. Ronaldo jumped forward and punched the ball past Lama. It was a goal! The Spanish supporters yelled in delight.

In the second half, PSG turned up the pressure but could not score. Barcelona triumphed. It was Ronaldo's first major title, and he coped well with the pressure of the big game.

Despite his great success in Spain, or maybe because of it, Ronaldo transferred to the Inter Milan club in Italy for the 1997–98 season. He had been so good that many of the top teams wanted him. His agents were anxious to make more profits, for they received one-tenth of his income, and that surely would rise with a new team.

After a long and very complicated negotiation—Barcelona accused Inter of illegally signing Ronaldo—Inter completed a $30 million transfer for the striker. Then, they signed him to a contract that guaranteed him $2.9 million a year until 2006, and they also gave him at least $10 million (some reports said it was $14 million) as a bonus. No other player could have received such a high-paying, long-term deal.

In the end, the transfer had been a business decision, not a personal one. Ronaldo realized that the Italian league was home to the greatest defenders of all, and he could not be sure of achieving the same level of success there. But he spoke bravely about the move.

"Everyone tells me that the Italian championship is the toughest in the world, but I'm not afraid. My life has always been a series of challenges, and I'm psychologically prepared, but this is the biggest challenge of my life."

The young star was sad to leave Barcelona but excited about moving to Milan, the heart of northern Italy. An ancient city, it was home to two of the most storied teams in soccer, Inter and AC Milan. Both had won major championships like the Cup-Winners Cup and the Champions Cup. In Milan, it was easy to want to succeed, for the entire city had a reputation for excellence. The Milanese were renowned as business leaders, fashion designers, publishers and advertisers. Ronaldo would fit in well with these over-achievers.

If Ronaldo thought the Spanish were passionate about soccer, he soon discovered that the Italians were obsessed with it. His picture graced the cover of every Italian sports magazine. In one day, all three national newspapers wrote full-page articles on him. One concentrated on Suzanna, another analyzed his performance with the Brazilian team, while the third discussed the new official Ronaldo site on the Internet.

When he finally jogged on the Inter field in San Siro stadium 45 minutes before his first match, 50,000 people gave Ronaldo a standing ovation, and fireworks streaked into the sky. Everywhere he went in Italy, large crowds of ecstatic fans greeted him. Many of the children had their heads shaved as a tribute to him. One teenage fan, trapped in such a mob, was heard to shout: "Ronaldo! You will save us! Say you will save us!"

Expectations were very high, partly because of Inter's cross-town rivalry with AC. Inter had fallen behind in the race, and everyone thought Ronaldo would single-handedly carry his team to the top. Because he was so famous, he also gave Inter an avalanche of good publicity, which in turn led to higher profits.

Ronaldo's financial impact on the team began to be felt immediately. After Ronaldo signed with the team, sales of season tickets jumped by 41 percent. Sports economist Marco Brunelli estimated that although Inter had invested at least $110 million to capture Ronaldo, the team would earn over twice that amount during the next eight years as a result of his presence.

It wasn't enough for Ronaldo to just show up on the field, however. Inter expected him to attend promotional events, dinners, public rallies—anything that would help the team's popularity.

Then there were his own business deals as well. Pirelli, the tire company that sponsored Inter, signed a marketing contract with Ronaldo worth $1.1 million a year after taxes. Brahma, the Brazilian beer manufacturers, and Parmalat, a food company, both sponsored him for just over half a million. As a very occasional drinker and the son of a recovering drinker, Ronaldo's deal with Brahma was strange. But it showed that when large amounts of money are involved, not to mention ambitious agents like Martins and Pitta, it is hard to say no.

All of these commitments made Ronaldo a very busy man. He traveled with three portable phones, and he always seemed to be talking to someone, usually his mother or his agents. Ronaldo was so popular with journalists that Inter claimed it would take a year-and-a-half of constant work for him to satisfy all the interview requests.

Constantly dealing with people made Ronaldo worldly, older than his 21 years. He now understood that almost everyone he met wanted something from him. His celebrity made it hard for him to trust people, but it complicated his day-to-day life as well. A simple act like leaving his four-bedroom apartment in San Siro, near the stadium, was difficult. The paparazzi—photographers who follow the rich and famous—were never far away. In Rio, Ronaldo used his brother to fool them, for Nelinho looked almost exactly like him. He would send Nelinho out to draw the paparazzi's attention, then slip away himself.

Another problem was the fact that he drove a Ferrari or a BMW in Milan, both expensive and high-powered cars. They were easy to recognize, and so was he. At traffic lights, people often gathered to stare and point at him. Ronaldo loved to drive, but the public made it hard for him to do it. They also prevented Ronaldo from going out to a movie, buying one of the North American-style hamburgers he loved, or doing anything else an ordinary person could do. If he had tried, he would have been mobbed.

Ronaldo knew this from experience. In the summer of 1997, he had gone to New York City in the United States. Enjoying the fact that he could wander the streets without being noticed—America did not follow his sport—he accidentally walked into Little Brazil, the area where most of the Brazilians in New York lived. He was surrounded by excited fans in an instant. "They were all going crazy," he recalled.

On the occasions when he wasn't playing, traveling or fulfilling business contracts, it was easier to stay home with Suzanna, who now lived with him. He was a multi-millionaire, but he did not live like one. With only a basic education, Ronaldo had simple tastes. He liked to explore the Internet on his computer, reading reviews of his play in the electronic newspapers. He liked to listen to one of the hundreds of music discs he owned, or just watch television. He did things that relaxed him and turned off his mind.

Having a passive, quiet personality, Ronaldo did not complain about the problems of fame. He simply withdrew. No one knew how much pressure he felt or how he was coping with it. Only rarely did he let his feelings loose, usually by breaking into tears. Once, during a film session, he showed a different side. Standing on the Copacabana Beach in his hometown, he was asked to show off his ball-juggling skills. Over and over again, he twirled the ball on his toes and bounced it off his thighs. Occasionally, when he lost control and it rolled into the ocean, he dived in to retrieve it.

Ronaldo went through this mind-numbing routine for three hours, getting cold and tired, but the film-makers still wanted more. Ronaldo stopped, strode over to the director and lectured him angrily. He was not a machine or a circus performer, but people often treated him that way.

Within two years, Ronaldo had shifted from an excellent player who was relatively unknown to a superstar who was recognized around the world. His life had been turned upside-down. The effect of such dramatic change had to come out sometime, and when it did, it surely would be more than a few angry words.

Former Brazilian soccer superstar Pele, center, with Ronaldo (left) and Roberto Carlos, poses with the FIFA player of the year trophy at the awards ceremony in France in January 1998. Ronaldo had won the award for the second year in a row, while fellow Brazilian Carlos came second.

Ronaldo tiumphantly displays the trophy after his team Inter Milan beat Lazio Roma 3–0 to win the UEFA Cup in Paris in 1998.

Ronaldo dribbles between Scotland's Colin Hendry (left) and John Collins during the opening game of World Cup 98 at the Stade de France. Brazil would win the game 2–1.

Ronaldo is challenged from behind by Frank Leboeuf of France during the final game of the World Cup in 1998. Ronaldo had suffered some sort of collapse before the game. Later there would be much debate about whether or not he should have been allowed to play.

Chapter 4

Playing the Game

October 12, 1996. Ronaldo, playing for Barcelona against Santiago de Compostela, takes control of the soccer ball. He glances at the opposing goal, 55 long yards (50 m) away.

As he begins to dribble the ball, a defender sweeps in from behind and trips him. Recovering his balance in a flash, Ronaldo starts to power his way downfield. The desperate opponent grabs Ronaldo's jersey, but the striker does not slow down. The defender is towed along for yards; then Ronaldo tosses him loose.

Four other opponents race to intercept Ronaldo. With a series of feints and dekes, he fools the first, the second, the third . . . Ronaldo slides around the last defender and into the penalty area, 18 yards (16.5 m) from the goal line. But he oversteps the ball; it is now behind him. Spinning in a circle, he collects the ball and shoots without a pause. The shot is so powerful that he tumbles backward to the ground.

The Compostela crowd roars. He has scored! On the sidelines, Barcelona coach Bobby Robson leaps up, staring into the crowd. Then, he looks back at Ronaldo, who is being mobbed by his teammates. "Oh my God!" Robson says. "Unbelievable."

Only 20, Ronaldo had scored one of the greatest goals of the decade. Yet, days later, he scored three times against Valencia, and each one was only a little less spectacular than the Compostela miracle. Goals such as these turn videotapes of Ronaldo highlights into bestsellers; in fact, his sell much more than other soccer tapes. No one else can do what Ronaldo does.

The Santiago goal revealed what made Ronaldo unique. He is often compared to Pele—the greatest soccer player in history—for his goal production, but his game is very different from Pele's. It is mainly a new style that does not follow in the Brazilian tradition. Pele was the ideal version of the Brazilian forward, the man who symbolized the stylish creativity of his country's game.

No other nation seemed to produce footballers like Brazil. While countries like England and Scotland played tough, efficient and defensive games, Brazil played as if it wanted to make fans faint in disbelief.

Pele was the ideal attacker, for all of his technical abilities were above criticism. He also had a gift for reading how a play was developing, and he would direct his teammates as he pleased. They were elevated by his mere presence, for he acted like a general on the field. More than anything, though, Pele was an unselfish player who was content to set up teammates if they had a better chance of scoring than himself.

The way Pele put his talents to use was also characteristic of his national style. Short and quick, he fired through defenses like an arrow or snaked around them cunningly, and he always seemed to be moving.

Footballers such as Pele inspired observers to comment that Brazilians play like samba dancers in the Rio carnival, that great, annual celebration of life which lasts four days. Samba, a music native to Brazil, was born in the favelas, just as Ronaldo was. At first, samba mournfully represented the sadness and suffering of the poor, but it gradually evolved to celebrate love and local culture. The basic passion for life found in Brazilians filtered into the music, made it heavily rhythmical and joyous. Samba dancers are elegant, skillful and hypnotizing. So was Pele.

Ronaldo, on the other hand, does not remind anyone of a dancer. His body, big and thick, is unusual for a Brazilian player. Six feet tall (183 cm) and 180 pounds (82 kg), he seems to be earthbound, for he does not leap for balls much, and he is only mediocre with his headers. But when he jogs down the pitch, he looks like a tank rumbling through a battlefield before it attacks.

And, when he explodes into top gear, Ronaldo resembles one of the BMWs or Ferraris that he enjoys driving. He becomes a sportscar. His acceleration is so great that the shoe which Nike designed for him, the Mercurial, is very light and flexible. That way, it allows for sudden movements.

Endurance is another of Ronaldo's machine-like qualities. He does not simply run at top speed for a few yards; he does so for prolonged distances. Over one-third or half the field, no other footballer can match him.

Ronaldo's ability to outlast opponents became clear during his career in Brazil. For instance, in April 1994, Ronaldo took to the pitch for Cruzeiro against Boca Juniors. At one point, he found himself at midfield with the ball. An entire team of defenders stood waiting for him.

Ronaldo began to dribble downfield. His teammates advanced alongside him, expecting a pass that never came. Sidestepping tackles, creating space with dekes that he invented as he ran, Ronaldo weaved towards the goal. No one could stop him. He blasted the ball past the goalie and ran yelling towards the sidelines with his arms stretched out—the pose that follows all of his goals. The country was amazed.

Apart from Ronaldo's long-distance dashes, coach Bobby Robson noted that "he's fabulous working in small spaces in the penalty box." This is something Ronaldo shares with Pele: the ability to control the ball among a mass of defenders. In Italy, where everyone played tight defense, where up to six opponents were assigned to stop him, Ronaldo still notched 34 goals in 1997–98.

Deception plays a key part in Ronaldo's style. He can shift his head to the right, as if he's running that way, then slip around a defender in the opposite direction. He executes the move quickly, so the opponent cannot adjust, and he can do three or four such moves with his head or body without losing the ball. His ability to turn instantly is remarkable.

While most players are left-footed or right-footed, Ronaldo shoots equally well with both. His shot, powerful, heavy and accurate, is even more dangerous because of this, for he can release it at any time. He does not have to receive a pass with one foot and then shoot with another, a move that requires an extra second. In soccer, these moments are crucial because they give defenders time to react.

Like Pele and the other greats, Ronaldo has the ability to be creative. Pele described it this way: "I feel the divine gift to make something out of nothing." For example, Ronaldo's goal against Compostela started innocently, near midfield. Normally, a player who took the ball at that point would dribble it for a short distance and then pass to a teammate, hoping to build an attack. Not Ronaldo. He wanted to score, as he always does, and though he didn't know how he would do it, he invented a way.

"The Phenomenon," as the Italian media termed

Ronaldo, is criticized for being too selfish with the ball, not using his teammates well enough and ignoring defensive responsibilities. Starting in San Cristovao, several of his coaches tried to change him, but Ronaldo would just smile, passively dismissing their advice.

On a Brazilian team, Ronaldo's style is out of place, for Brazilians use a sustained, group attack. They make constant, short passes downfield and gradually increase pressure on their opponent. When they are close to the goal, they weave back and forth until the best moment to shoot arrives.

This patient approach does not suit Ronaldo. He wants results immediately. Yet, once he has put himself into position to score, he does not look impatient. He takes his time and calmly decides what to do. He knows that this is one moment he cannot rush.

To call Ronaldo selfish is not entirely fair. He has an intense drive to finish plays that marks him as a great goal scorer. Nothing else gives him the same satisfaction. He wants to be the center of attention, the one who decides a game. His style is unusual, even rebellious, but it works. When he joined Inter, the club was smart enough to leave him alone.

"As long as I keep my scoring numbers high, they let me do what I like to do," Ronaldo commented.

Another trait Ronaldo has in common with Pele is passion, the most important one of all. The

Portuguese word he uses to describe it is *alegria*. Translated, it means "deep joy." To be as focused as Ronaldo is, you must love and enjoy the game. In childhood, soccer was almost the only bright light in his life, and he poured all of his energy into it. That was how he became great and why he stayed at that level, no matter the opposition or the weather.

In the 1998 UEFA Cup semifinals, Inter played against Spartak in Moscow, Russia, under the most challenging conditions. The city was filled with snow and the field was a muddy mess. When the ball gets wet and muddy, it becomes heavy and hard to control. But even in the cold, which he dislikes, and on a bad pitch, Ronaldo still managed to score—twice. His effort was hailed by soccer fans around the world.

As a child, Ronaldo first had to play the game of soccer forcefully, since others would not pass him the ball. As he matured, he refined this element. When Ronaldo charges downfield, he does not worry about physical contact. Often, he simply bulls through forwards, midfielders and fullbacks, knowing that his size and strength give him the upper hand. Not many forwards could drag a defender along, as Ronaldo did against Compostela. Since no one wants to run into Ronaldo, his approach creates fear among opponents. Mentally, he has the advantage as soon as he steps on the field.

When Ronaldo does not have the ball, he relaxes

and floats around. You do not notice him. But when the moment is right, he appears to seize the ball and confuse startled defenders. He may go an entire match without touching the ball, then score in the 90th minute to create a victory.

Ronaldo does not dominate all the time, as Pele did, but his unpredictable play makes him just as dangerous in his own way. He is like a magician who shows up unexpectedly, performs a beautiful trick, and vanishes again.

More than anything, Ronaldo is a new type of player. He has the finesse of a Brazilian, but his physical play echoes that of the Germans or the English. In an era when players move around the world's leagues with ease, regardless of nationality, Ronaldo symbolizes football's current age.

Chapter 5

World Cup Goals

Days after scoring into his own net, a goal that accidentally helped to eliminate his team from World Cup
94, Andres Escobar was outside a restaurant in his
native Colombia. Suddenly, a barrage of gunshots
shattered the air. Escobar was killed.

While the world mourned for this victim of soccer
extremism, the incident showed just how emotionally
crazed people can become during the World Cup.
Since it is the most popular game, soccer is the one
sporting event—aside from the Olympics—that
defines where a country stands. If you win the World
Cup, your nation feels like a champion. If you lose or
play poorly, there is shame, anger and endless ques-
tioning across the country. More than anything, in the
World Cup teams play for national pride, not a trophy.

When each World Cup tournament begins, once
every four years, it signals the end of normal, every-
day existence for soccer fans around the globe. People
forget about school or work. Family life often becomes
an afterthought. Essentials such as food or sleep may

be ignored. There is a saying that captures this attitude: "Soccer is not a matter of life and death; it's more serious than that."

On the day of its opening match against Scotland in World Cup 98, Brazil declared a holiday. Most government activities halted, and banks, schools and shops closed. Hospitals tried to cope with fewer doctors and nurses. Judges announced they would not oversee court cases until the final was over, provided Brazil made it that far. It might have been a good time for criminals to strike, but in Brazil, even lawbreakers were busy watching their soccer heroes. The retired Brazilian star Pele, with his famous wit, had the best view of the situation: "After God comes soccer in Brazil."

Meanwhile, politicians tried to please voters by installing televisions in rural villages and isolated settlements in the Amazon jungle. A massive screen sprung up in the center of Rio so that the poor and homeless could see the games. It was clear that World Cup fever made the authorities more charitable than usual. If Brazil won, who could say what they would give away?

Along with the excitement came intense pressure. With four World Cup titles, Brazil had the best record in history, and its people only expected to win. Many experts also picked Brazil as the favorite, although Argentina, France, the Netherlands and one or two more were very strong. Anything less than a championship would be bitterly disappointing for Brazilians.

At the center of the pressure stood Ronaldo. As Brazil's biggest star and main goal scorer, he was expected to be team leader, even though Dunga, the tough veteran, actually captained the squad.

Ronaldo had lived up to the incredibly high expectations of his first season in Italy. He was named FIFA World Player of the Year for 1997, clearly winning over Brazilian teammate Roberto Carlos. Ronaldo became the first man to capture the award twice in a row.

Then, he finished as the league's second-best scorer and guided Inter to the UEFA Cup championship. In the final, played in Paris's Parc des Princes stadium, Ronaldo scored once in a 3-0 win over Lazio and was named player of the game. He had won in the very city where World Cup 98 would begin and end. Surely it was a good omen; fate seemed to be blessing him.

The pressure on Ronaldo could be summarized by looking at an advertisement he did for the Pirelli tire company in February 1998. In Rio, there is a giant statue of Jesus Christ that looks down on the city from Corcovado mountain. Pirelli decided to create a poster of this scene, but it replaced Christ's image with one of Ronaldo in his Inter uniform. The message was clear: just as Christians hailed Jesus as their savior, Ronaldo was supposed to save his team with his nearly divine skill.

As the tournament approached, journalists everywhere predicted Ronaldo would dominate it. They analyzed his talents and retold the stories of his sad childhood and rapid rise to stardom. They couldn't stop talking about him. Even in North America, where soccer is not yet a very popular spectator sport, people began to know Ronaldo's name.

In May, once the regular soccer season had ended, the Brazilian team set up a training camp in the small town of Lesigny, France, just outside Paris. The 8,000 residents suddenly found themselves invaded by 2,000 fans and journalists, all following in the wake of the national squad like seagulls behind a fishing boat. The team found sanctuary and a temporary home within the white walls of the Château de la Grande Romaine, a large hotel built in a pleasant meadow.

In the neighboring town of Ozoir-La-Ferriere, the cramped main street was filled with small shops, open markets and cafés, all decorated in green and golden yellow, the Brazilian team colors. At the end of the road stood Municipal Stadium, a humble building where the team practiced.

The town was usually pretty quiet, but when Ronaldo and his peers were inside Municipal Stadium, the main street was jammed with cars. The stands in the stadium filled with fans and writers. As each player walked onto the field, the fans chanted his name loudly, paced by a drummer or a trumpeter. Hundreds of journalists watched as the players juggled balls with their feet or their heads, spinning them endlessly with no obvious effort. When coach Mario Zagallo ran them through their drills, cameras flashed and a television commentator fired out phrases in Portuguese, describing the scenes as if they were part of a real match.

Ronaldo seemed fine to the observers, but his mother and his coaches were worried about him. In December, the national team had traveled to Saudi Arabia for the Confederations Cup, an eight-team tournament. Brazil destroyed the Australians 6-0 to win the event.

However, the real drama happened off the field when Ronaldo read a gloomy newspaper article about himself. The writer predicted that unless Ronaldo began to cut back on his incredibly busy schedule, he would burn out and lose control, just as soccer super-star Maradona had. Though Maradona had reached the top, winning a World Cup with Argentina, his life had become a tragic story of drug abuse and wasted potential.

After reading this article, the calm face of Little Buddha rippled into tears. He could not stop crying, for he suddenly felt the journalist could be right. Teammate Cesar Sampaio tried to comfort him, but Ronaldo was inconsolable.

"We can all learn from what happened to Maradona," Ronaldo told him between sobs.

Sonia saw another side of her son. As France 98 approached—each tournament is named for its host country—Ronaldo became silent and distant. This was not how he usually acted around her. Normally, Ronaldo was gentle, affectionate and playful. She knew he was reacting against the great pressure building on his shoulders, the expectation that he would carry Brazil to victory. Sonia insisted he rent a house in Paris during the tournament. That way, she and Suzanna—who now was engaged to Ronaldo—would be close to him in case anything went wrong.

Ronaldo left Italy to join the Brazilian national team on May 24. He arrived at Charles de Gaulle airport in Paris late in the evening, but he did not show up at Lesigny on time. Knowing that he was in a fragile state, Coach Zagallo and his associates wondered if Ronaldo had lost his courage and fled back to Rio.

Ronaldo did arrive, but he was several hours late and he was almost in hysterics. Team doctor Lidio Toledo gave him a tranquilizer, a pill that would relax his body and mind.

When he had calmed down a bit, Ronaldo explained that he had expected a team representative to meet him at the airport. When nobody appeared, he took a taxi. The driver lost his way to Lesigny, causing a long delay. By themselves, these events were not very odd. Ronaldo must have been feeling a lot of stress to react so deeply to them.

Fatigue was part of his problem. The Italian season had been his biggest challenge so far. From beginning to end, Ronaldo had needed all of his strength to cope with, and then triumph over, the intense, prolonged demands. The public had asked for a championship. He had supplied it, and now he deserved a holiday. Instead, he was thrown right back into the race with a nearly-empty gas tank.

While Ronaldo was dreading the start of the World Cup tournament, few others felt the same. France was a beautiful and romantic setting for the world's biggest sports event. Its capital, Paris, was built in the rich soil of a northern lowland. A well-known line says Paris is like a woman with flowers in her hair. The "flowers" were the parks and small forests, over one dozen, that filled the famous city. Inside, visitors found towering trees, wide, multi-colored flower beds and smooth, well-cut grass stretching for miles. Even the large avenues that swarmed with traffic were graced by high chestnut trees.

Paris was the site of the opening ceremonies, and the Cup's organizing committee had invented a parade that would catch the eye of any citizen. On June 9, the procession began with 4,500 participants marching towards the center of Paris from its outlying corners. Four plastic giants, 65 feet (20 metres) high, led each group, gliding at one mile an hour (1.5 km/h). Made to represent races from Africa, Asia,

Europe and the Americas, the giants' feet were constructed from trucks, allowing them to drive along the avenues.

Behind the giants strode performers dressed as dragons, huge insects, tropical baobab trees, orange eyeballs, fish . . . there was even a group of tiny pygmies from Cameroon in Africa. These were not people dressed as pygmies, but real ones. The committee had thought of everything.

As the performers danced along, hundreds of thousands of fans lined the sidewalks, waving and cheering. Behind them, close to 2,000 stern-faced soldiers patrolled the streets, looking for signs of danger. A terrorist group might have picked the World Cup as a target for a bombing or an assassination, for they knew everyone would be watching.

The parade moved on, eventually ending at the Place de la Concorde or Square of Peace. It was an appropriately named meeting place: no one had ruined the show with violence.

Since they were defending champions, the Brazilians were picked to play the opening game on June 10. Every team began the tournament in one of eight groups. Each group had four teams, all of whom played each other once.

Brazil was in a relatively easy group with Norway, Scotland and Morocco. Scotland was its first opponent: a tough and disciplined team, but one that lacked goal-scoring. Ronaldo should have been confident entering the battle.

However, coach Mario Zagallo had lectured him about the dangers of opposing defenders. One of them could injure him easily with a reckless tackle. His agents and his employers at Inter also were expecting him to avoid rough play. They simply had too much money invested in him.

Already worried, Ronaldo took these warnings to heart. The man who specialized in running through opponents was concerned about running away from them now.

The superstar also was preoccupied by his personal life. Photographers had captured Ronaldo giving a polite kiss to Anna Kournikova, a beautiful tennis player. The picture was printed in a Rio newspaper, and when his fiancée Suzanna saw it, she was furious. She called Ronaldo at the team chateau, and they yelled and argued about it. The incident marked the start of a difficult period in their relationship.

While Suzanna could be possessive, as the Kournikova incident showed, so could Ronaldo. He hated the fact that Suzanna had to kiss men in the films and television shows she had begun to appear in. They were only make-believe kisses, but that made no difference to Ronaldo. He wanted her to stop. She didn't want to. It was another subject they argued about a lot.

The after-effects of his parents' divorce also troubled Ronaldo in Paris. He had rented a house for his father in the city, but Nelio and Ronaldo's mother Sonia could not stand to be in the same room. Both had remarried, but they had failed to heal the wounds of Nelio's irresponsible behavior. Ronaldo had to keep them in opposite ends of the city. The strain of reliving the most traumatic part of his childhood—his parents' divorce—was hard to handle.

Hours before the Scotland match, Ronaldo's many anxieties bubbled to the surface. In his room, he broke into tears and began shaking. Only his teammates saw it happen, and they kept it a secret from the coaches. They didn't realize how serious the problem was, and they didn't want to embarrass him. Ronaldo was left alone, but not in peace.

With an unhappy star in their midst, the Brazilians boarded a bus and rode to St-Denis, a suburb of Paris. There, amidst grimy factories and ugly industrial plants, the magnificent bowl of the Stade de France rose up, its glass and steel frame sparkling in the summer sun. The stadium had been erected especially for the World Cup. Now it was filled with just over 80,000 noisy soccer fans.

The Brazilian supporters, dressed in eye-catching yellows and greens, waved huge flags and pounded thunderously on their samba drums. One was dressed as a nun; a few more wore pumpkins on their heads.

The Scots—better known as the "Tartan Army"—competed for attention with gigantic, ginger-colored wigs and loud blasts from bagpipes. Male Scottish fans wore kilts, short, dress-like outfits that symbolize their culture. When the Scots discovered that air streams from ventilation grilles made their kilts fly up, they marched back and forth over them in delight.

The day before, Parisians had learned just how wild the Scots could be. Swarms of them ran into the streets, halting traffic as they made a good-natured fuss. Even more flocked to the bars and clubs, where they drank lots and lots of beer and sang patriotic songs. On the subway, the natives stared unemotionally at the Scots as they celebrated, but it was impossible to dislike them. They were harmless.

The Brazilians showed themselves too, forming lines, swaying happily to the beat of their drums, smiling broadly. If the Scots met the Brazilians, they shook hands and celebrated together. Both nationalities showed the World Cup spirit at its finest.

A few minutes before kickoff, the Brazilian team ran on the field to the screams and whistles of its fans. There was Taffarel, the goalie; Cafu, Aldair, Junior Baiano and Roberto Carlos, the fullbacks; Cesar Sampaio, Giovanni, Dunga and Rivaldo, the midfielders; and the strikers, Ronaldo and Bebeto. As he always did, Ronaldo made the sign of the cross.

Scotland appeared. The teams exchanged gifts,

then stood at attention as their national anthems echoed through the stadium speakers. Jogging out to their positions, they waited as referee José Maria Garcia Aranda blew his whistle to start the match. Scotland's Gordon Durie tapped the ball to a teammate, and the World Cup began.

Brazil looked mediocre throughout much of the game, but it scored two lucky goals. One went in off Sampaio's shoulder as he attempted a header, while the other bounced off two Scottish players before rebounding into the net. Scotland, with little attacking flair, took its lone goal on a penalty shot. At the finish, the relieved Brazilians danced around the field. They had not dominated, so they were fortunate to win.

There were many reasons behind Brazil's unimpressive show. Brazilian footballers were well-known for their individualistic ways, and this team was no exception. Reserve striker Edmundo, better known as "the Animal," once had assaulted a referee, earning a four-month suspension. He also liked to brawl with coaches, opponents and teammates—especially Junior Baiano. Ronaldo disliked Edmundo a lot. Edmundo wanted to play in place of Bebeto, but it was clear he wouldn't suit Ronaldo.

Bebeto, considered relatively normal, had deserted the national team in 1991, only to return. His partnership with Ronaldo began at the 1996 Olympics, but it did not work. After leading Nigeria 3-1 in the semifinals, Brazil collapsed and lost the game, later settling for a bronze medal. Bebeto complained that Ronaldo never gave up the ball, while Ronaldo stated that the Olympic team's problem was leadership—which many interpreted to mean Bebeto's leadership.

The two had apologized to each other, but Ronaldo missed his hero, Romario. The star of World Cup 94, Romario was a great playmaker who engineered his team's offense. He would have played in France, but an injury forced him to leave the team at the last minute. Ronaldo was very upset by the news. Now, he alone would decide the fate of Brazil's offense.

With all of these tensions, Brazil had not played well since 1998 began. The team was not scoring goals and it looked uninspired. The media in Rio were angry and outraged. One disadvantage to being defending champion was that Brazil qualified automatically for World Cup 98. Except for the host country, every other nation had to play qualifying matches over a two-year span. Only the best survived. Brazil had to play exhibitions and small tournaments where little was at stake. It was hard to stay sharp that way.

After the match against Scotland, Ronaldo went to his rented house, even though Coach Zagallo wanted the team to stay isolated in the chateau. A Brazilian film crew had asked to take pictures of him and Suzanna at home.

But when they arrived, one of the crew members,

Pedro Bial, realized that the couple had been fighting. The atmosphere felt tense and Ronaldo was wearing a shirt with these words on it: "Don't look at me, my girlfriend is jealous." The Kournikova incident had not been forgotten.

Still, there were important games to think about. The next challenge for Brazil was Morocco. The two teams faced off in Nantes on June 16. A small port city in western France, Nantes lay in one of the more barren and rugged sections of the country. But the Brazilians found something that reminded them of home: the city had built a replica of the Copacabana Beach to welcome them.

Encouraged by the support, Brazil blossomed in front of 33,266 delighted spectators. Suddenly, the players were passing fluidly and weaving around Moroccans as if they didn't exist. Rivaldo set up Ronaldo for the opening goal, and the striker punched it in easily from 18 yards (16.5 m) for his first World Cup marker. Then, Rivaldo ran in close to the goal line and scored himself after taking a cross from Cafu.

The third and final goal showed Ronaldo at his best. Seizing a loose ball near the sideline, he changed speeds quickly and dribbled expertly around two Moroccans. Another spun the wrong way, and Ronaldo was running into empty space. The goaltender came out to challenge him. Ronaldo slid the ball across to Bebeto, who tapped it into the empty net.

Still, there was one unhappy moment. Dunga thought Bebeto had been slow to defend against a free kick, and he criticized him sharply. Bebeto stepped up to him angrily, and Leonardo had to jump in between them before it turned ugly. Even in a 3-0 victory, the team did not look unified.

The breach seemed to be healed when Dunga and Bebeto shook hands after the game. But, a few days later, a report said that Dunga had thrown down his captain's armband at a team meeting and offered to resign unless he was treated with respect. The team apparently voted to keep him as its leader.

Since the start of the tournament, many rumors had been circulating about the team's unhappiness. The Brazilian media had discovered that Ronaldo wasn't happy, but was he unfit as well? People whispered about his knee. They claimed he was receiving injections in it.

This was the same leg that he had wrecked during his second season with PSV. In a practice, Ronaldo had fractured the tibia just below his knee. He had returned home to Rio to heal. Trainer Nelson Petroni, who gave him a series of exercises to strengthen the joint, believed the injury was a result of his youth. Ronaldo was growing rapidly at the time, and that placed stress on his body parts. Petroni warned him that unless he continued the exercises, he could face further injuries.

Now, Ronaldo's knee felt sore again. He was suffering from tendonitis, an inflammation of the tendons that held his knee muscles to the bone. To make matters worse, a Moroccan had tackled him violently in their game. The defender brought his shoe down hard across Ronaldo's thigh, and Ronaldo discovered he had two injuries to deal with.

He didn't tell the media much about the thigh problem, as Zagallo instructed, and he denied that he had received any knee injections, calling the rumor "a joke in bad taste." The knee problem was minor, he said, and it would not restrict his play.

After the Morocco match, stories about Ronaldo and Suzanna erupted into public view. Suzanna was working for Brazilian television, covering the Cup, and one of her colleagues was Pedro Bial, who had interviewed the couple days earlier. Now some people claimed she was having a romance with Bial. Soon after, an Argentinean newspaper wrote a piece that echoed this rumor. It was totally untrue, and Ronaldo knew it.

Meanwhile, Brazilian newspapers had accused Suzanna of intentionally missing a meeting with her boyfriend. Other reports said they had broken up and he had thrown away his engagement ring.

Ronaldo was angry as he spoke to the media about it: "I am used to people trying to break my concentration. . . . Of course, it hurts me that some people want to lash out at me. . . . Every time I do something, they turn it round and it becomes a bad taste story." In fact, Ronaldo later admitted that he had split up with Suzanna for two days.

Even when he stayed in the room he shared with Roberto Carlos, Ronaldo could not find peace. Carlos and several other teammates practiced macumba, the African-descended religion that had evolved in Brazil. Devotees of macumba believe in many gods and frequently practice intense magic rituals. The witch doctor who predicted Ronaldo's greatness had been a macumba master.

Ronaldo had seen some macumba rituals as a child, for his family sometimes practiced it. Once, he had been so frightened by an eerie ceremony that he ran away from the house. But his family's main belief system was Roman Catholicism, which explained his habit of crossing himself before every game. Before the World Cup, he had visited the Pope, the leader of the Roman Catholic faith. The famous priest had blessed Ronaldo's national team jersey. Ronaldo would not part with it, for he believed it would bring him good luck.

Ronaldo was not used to living with someone who believed in macumba completely. Carlos carried good luck charms wherever he went, and he set up a shrine in the room so he could pray to his gods. He lectured Ronaldo about the importance of pleasing the gods and the unseen spirits. Many, many things could trigger their anger, he warned.

Listening to all of this serious talk, Ronaldo became even more nervous. He did not want to think about whether his problems had been caused by unhappy spirits.

Brazil's next opponent was Norway. The previous year, Norway had surprised Brazil with a 4-2 win in an exhibition game. Deep inside, the Norwegians knew they had a chance to do it again in Marseilles, the oldest city in France. Perched on the Mediterranean Sea, Marseilles had been built in the warmest and most attractive part of the country. It was the direct opposite of Nantes.

The match turned out to be the reverse of the Nantes clash with Morocco as well. Brazil couldn't seem to do anything right in the first half. When Rivaldo and Ronaldo managed to set up Cafu with a pretty play, he sailed the ball past the net. As for the Norwegians, they defended well but kept missing their chances in the Brazilian penalty area.

With only 12 minutes left in the game, Bebeto scored, but the desperate Norwegians rallied. Tore Andre Flo sent a brilliant, curving shot past Taffarel to tie the score. Then, Goncalves pushed Flo in the penalty box and the referee surprisingly awarded a penalty shot to Norway. Kjetil Rekdal booted the ball into the net. Brazil was stunned, while the Norwegian fans celebrated wildly. The remaining two minutes ticked by, and Norway survived.

It was a shocking upset. Afterwards, Zagallo was humble in defeat. "We came in overconfident," he said. "But we developed and will continue to do so."

What the Brazilian coach didn't mention was that Ronaldo had been afraid to push himself because of his injuries. No one knew whether he could reach full speed if he had to.

Ronaldo had three days of rest before taking the field against Chile in the Parc des Princes, the stadium where he had captured the UEFA Cup. From now on, every round was a one-game, sudden-death affair. Whoever lost this second-round match would fly home with a sad heart.

But for the first time, Brazil showed up in its full glory. Ronaldo scored twice, once on a penalty, and drove Chile berserk with his clever runs. The rest of the team looked inspired by him, and Brazil coasted to a 4-1 win.

Before his quarter-final battle with Denmark, Ronaldo again admitted to a journalist that his knee was not healthy, but he called it a "slight pain" that occurred when he sprinted or stopped quickly. He also said that he missed Romario as a partner up front.

But when he took to the field in Nantes on July 3, it looked as if Ronaldo had decided to play like Romario. In the 11th minute, with Brazil down 1-0,

Ronaldo saw Bebeto sneaking through the middle of the field. He sent a wonderful pass beyond the Danes that surprised them. Bebeto collected the ball, ran past a defender, and hit a perfect shot into the corner of the net.

Sixteen minutes later, Roberto Carlos stole the ball from a Dane. He passed to a waiting Ronaldo, who was flanked by Rivaldo in the middle. The two closed in on the goal. Recognizing that Rivaldo had a better angle to shoot, Ronaldo side-footed a fine pass into the penalty box. Rivaldo lifted it over Denmark's great goalie, Peter Schmeichel, who dived in vain.

Brazil needed this playmaking, for Denmark attacked courageously throughout. In the end, Rivaldo's goal in the 60th minute gave Brazil a thrilling win, 3-2.

Ronaldo's play impressed critics who had labeled him selfish and one-dimensional. He showed that the team did come first in his mind. He had created a good chemistry with Rivaldo during the tournament, but the team's offense was appearing and disappearing unpredictably. It seemed unable to attack for 90 minutes. As for the defense, everyone felt it was vulnerable, and Denmark's play confirmed this.

Brazil's next opponent was the Netherlands, who had survived a very close match with Argentina. The Dutch appeared to have the best team of all: well-balanced, creative, strong in goal. It was an ideal match that millions wanted to see, but only 54,000 lucky fans could cheer from the stands in Marseilles on July 7.

The first half was surprisingly tense and defensive, and both teams appeared to be nervous. Immediately after the second-half kickoff, Ronaldo slipped down the right side and grabbed a pass from Rivaldo. The Dutch were caught sleeping. Ronaldo was alone on a breakaway. He sped down the field as the Brazilian fans roared. Goalie Edwin van der Sar moved out to challenge, and Ronaldo calmly punched the ball past him. Like many of Ronaldo's goals, it seemed to come from nowhere.

The game then became lively and exciting. Van der Sar stopped Ronaldo from close range, while Brazil missed several other opportunities to take a 2-0 lead. At the other end, striker Patrick Kluivert threatened constantly, but he could not find the target with his shots. With only three minutes left, Kluivert rose to head an excellent cross. This time, he did not miss. Overtime beckoned.

In previous World Cups, the 30-minute overtime had been played to the end, regardless of who scored. Now, the first team to score would win. In the second round, against Paraguay, France had scored the first "golden goal" in Cup history as the country watched breathlessly in overtime.

Now, faced with the same fate as Paraguay, the Brazilians reached inside and lifted their game. They were champions and they had tremendous pride, even if they weren't always united. Almost immediately, Ronaldo, Denilson and Rivaldo grabbed the ball and ran towards van der Sar. Roberto Carlos, who attacked from his defense position better than anyone, arrowed up to support them. After taking a back pass, Carlos hooked a cross into the penalty box, where his forwards waited. Desperately, the goalie leaped to deflect it away, but the ball went straight to Ronaldo.

All of Brazil sat motionless. Would this be the deciding moment? Skillfully, Ronaldo measured his shooting angle and curved the ball towards the open net. Suddenly, there was fullback Frank de Boer, standing on the goal line. Just before the ball entered the net, de Boer booted it away.

A minute later, van der Sar somehow stopped another great shot from Little Buddha, who had charged around a defender. The Dutch sagged. Again and again, the Brazilians strode forward; again and again, the Dutch found a way to deny them.

Then, inspired by his tying goal, Kluivert tried for the winner. Breaking loose down the right side, he rocketed the ball inches wide of the far post as Taffarel watched, helpless.

Thirty minutes came and went in the flash of an eye. The whistle blew. Penalty kicks would decide the winner. The penalty shootout is the most cruel, unfair and thrilling moment in soccer. It is a test of skill rather than team play, so it doesn't always reward the strongest team. But it always decides a winner. Each team alternates five shooters, and the team with the most goals takes the game. Brazil had the tactical advantage of shooting first. If Brazil scored, the Netherlands would have to do the same.

Ronaldo stepped forward as the first shooter. The crowd turned quiet. In the streets of Brazil and the Netherlands, there was an unnatural silence. Not a person could be seen for miles. Almost every citizen of each country was inside, staring anxiously at a television screen. At the midfield line, the Dutch team stood arm in arm, each player sharing his strength with the next. The Brazilians lay exhausted on the pitch; they had run themselves into the ground.

Ronaldo confidently whipped the ball past van der Sar. It was a magnificent shot that could not be saved. Next, Frank de Boer came forth for the Dutch. He too was perfect. Rivaldo shot, then Dennis Bergkamp, then Emerson. Now Brazil led 3-2. Phillip Cocu, the next Dutch shooter, punched the ball to Taffarel's left, but it was too close to the goalie. He dived to push it away, then leaped up triumphantly. Now Brazil was ahead. Dunga then scored easily, which meant Ronald de Boer had to succeed. He pushed the ball uncertainly at the middle of the net. Taffarel blocked it. Coach Zagallo leaped off the bench and hugged his coaches as the team mobbed Taffarel. Brazil had won!

It was a great victory, but it came with a heavy price. Ronaldo's knee was suffering badly from the constant running. The entire team was worn out from the strain. It had found a way to beat a slightly superior opponent, and now it would have to find the energy to play the final in five days.

France, with superb defense and well-timed offense, reached the final as well, beating Croatia 2-1. About 350,000 fans poured into the streets of Paris, celebrating the win. The whole country would be against Brazil in the championship match.

The day before the final, Ronaldo left the team to see Suzanna. The players were supposed to be isolated, preparing for the match on their own, but he had to see her: the pressure of the Cup was almost at its peak. He made roommate Roberto Carlos promise not to tell anyone.

For days, Ronaldo had seemed tired and depressed. Sometimes, he did not appear to know what he was doing. He often quivered and shook. Carlos could not understand what was wrong. He knew Ronaldo and Suzanna had been fighting, but Ronaldo seemed to be turning into another person.

When Ronaldo reached Suzanna's rented house, he had another emotional breakdown. Just as he had done as a child, he cried in the face of fear. He could not stop crying, and Suzanna began to do the same. He told her he didn't care what people said about her, he just needed her at his side. Then he went back to his hotel room, but Suzanna phoned him in the evening to complain. She felt neglected, she said, because he only thought about soccer.

It was true that Ronaldo had been self-absorbed and remote for months. In this state, it was hard for him to be a good fiancé. Still, Suzanna had picked the worst moment to mention this. Her words sparked another fight.

Afterwards, as Ronaldo went to bed before the biggest game of his life, he was a deeply unhappy man. Just when he needed her, his wife-to-be had let him down.

The next afternoon, Ronaldo and Roberto Carlos were relaxing in their room. Many players were taking a pre-game nap. Around 2:00, Carlos heard strange sounds from his sleeping teammate. He looked over and saw a shocking sight. Ronaldo, now very pale, was convulsing uncontrollably. Sweat washed down his face and his arms and hands bulged grotesquely. He was gasping for air. Carlos ran out of the room, screaming for help.

Four teammates arrived immediately. "He's dead, he's dead!" someone yelled. The words echoed in the corridor, waking everyone. Carlos and Rivaldo began to cry. Team doctor Lidio Toledo rushed to the scene. Ronaldo's mouth was choked with saliva. When Toledo cleared it, Ronaldo began to breathe properly.

Now awake, he was confused and scared, but he seemed to be recovering.

Coach Zagallo met with the team doctors and discussed the bizarre situation. He decided that Ronaldo could not play that evening and announced that Edmundo would replace him. They sent Ronaldo into Paris so he could be tested at the Clinic des Lilas.

The rest of the team climbed on the bus and drove to the stadium in St-Denis. As they left, the players were totally silent. The manager of their chateau later said, "At that moment there was no cohesion and they had lost the Cup."

Normally, when a person suffers a fit like Ronaldo seemed to have had, there are physical after-effects. When Ronaldo was tested at the clinic, the doctors found nothing wrong. They said he appeared to be fine. Meanwhile, Zagallo submitted his official lineup to the game authorities, and he left Ronaldo's name off it. This meant Ronaldo could not play under the laws of FIFA, the International Association Soccer Federation.

But then Ronaldo arrived at the stadium, seemingly happy and relaxed, asking to play, and Zagallo changed his mind. At 8:15 p.m., he gave FIFA another lineup with Ronaldo's name, claiming that he had been trying to trick the French the first time. FIFA broke its own rules and allowed the superstar to take the field.

Many people speculated that the Nike company had played a role in this reversal. As the main sponsor of both Ronaldo and the Brazilian team, Nike had everything to lose if he did not show up in the final. The company had built its World Cup marketing strategy around Ronaldo. Nike ads featuring him were playing constantly on television worldwide. The public knew that the firm had a lot of influence over the Brazilian soccer federation, but just how much power did it really have? Could it control lineup decisions?

The answer was no. Zagallo made the decision by himself. Nike's expectations were just part of the enormous pressure on Ronaldo. Almost everyone, not only Nike, wanted to see him play. This was modern soccer, where tens of millions of dollars were invested in superstars and hundreds of millions in national teams. With giant expenditures came giant expectations.

Before the final, the atmosphere in the Brazilian dressing room was depressing. When the players first heard Ronaldo would not play, they were horrified. One report said they threatened to stay in the room if he didn't go out with them. Yet, after Zagallo changed his mind and wrote out a second lineup sheet, assistant coach Zico and a few teammates argued that Ronaldo had to stay out of the match.

Suddenly, Ronaldo was seized by nervousness. Dr. Toledo made a fateful decision to give him half of a tranquilizer pill 35 minutes before kickoff. Though his teammates didn't know it, Ronaldo began to drift into a haze. His muscles relaxed and his mind lost its focus.

As the teams took to the pitch in front of 75,000, Brazil was angry, upset and confused. Not one player was mentally ready for the match. Ronaldo's disturbed face betrayed his physical state. His Milan Inter teammate Youri Djorkaeff, one of the French players, noticed it immediately. He spoke to his friend and Ronaldo mumbled that he did not feel well.

France, on the other hand, was focused and confident. It had been building strength as the tournament progressed. Midfielder Zinedine Zidane, one of the world's best, had proven to be a fine leader.

As the Brazilians wandered around, trying to calm themselves, France attacked repeatedly. One minute in, Stephane Guivarc'h almost scored. After two more good chances, France took a corner kick in the 27th minute. Emmanuel Petit curled the ball in to Zidane, who headed it powerfully past Taffarel for the opening goal. The Brazilians barely moved to defend against him.

Then, just before halftime, Zidane scored again on a similar play. The French fans screamed passionately, almost in disbelief over its team's domination.

Throughout the game, as almost two billion people watched on television, Coach Zagallo wondered if he should remove Ronaldo. The striker had about three dangerous moments, but the rest of the time, he seemed to be sleepwalking as a result of the drug. Zagallo could not find the courage to take out his best player.

Meanwhile, France created several excellent chances, but each time, its strikers missed. Brazil could not score at all. With one minute left, Petit took off on a breakaway and celebrated the last goal of the World Cup.

By this time, the stadium was shaking with cheers. Confetti flew down from the stands and the French fans chanted in ecstasy. As the final whistle sounded, French goalie Fabien Barthez fell to the ground and covered his head. Petit and Frank Leboeuf also tumbled over. The rest of the players walked around in shock, crying and hugging each other. They were too stunned to celebrate.

In the stands, Suzanna covered her face with a Brazilian flag and cried for a different reason, knowing she had contributed to her boyfriend's defeat. Ronaldo cried as well. Brazil's reserve goalie, Dida, came over to comfort him as he stood with his head in his hands.

Outside, Paris was launching its biggest party since it had been liberated from the Germans in World War Two. Over one million people streamed into the Champs-Elysées—the city's great avenue—and ran under the Arc de Triomphe, the symbol of French military success built by Emperor Napoleon I in the 1800s.

Now the country had conquered the world in the

somewhat gentler pursuit of soccer. The fans jumped on cars, climbed telephone booths and did whatever came into their hearts. Horns blared. People screamed. The noise was overwhelming.

Afterwards, in the chateau, a guilty Ronaldo kept asking Carlos if he alone was the reason for the loss. He needed to feel blameless; he needed, finally, the pressure to lift. Carlos could not find any reassuring words for Ronaldo. The next day, though, Ronaldo sounded as if he had placed the game in perspective.

"We lost the World Cup, but I won something else—my life." He believed he had been close to death during his convulsion.

When the world learned of Ronaldo's fit—he announced it during an interview after first denying it—the story leaped onto the front pages of every newspaper. It even threatened to overshadow the French triumph.

Everyone had an opinion on the matter. An important English doctor, Adrian Williams, said it had been wrong for Ronaldo to play after such an attack. The owner of Inter Milan, Massimo Moratti, said the Brazilian team had made an absurd decision. Many wondered if Ronaldo had epilepsy, a serious brain disorder that can cause fits. But team doctor Lidio Toledo claimed Ronaldo had been suffering from nothing more than emotional stress.

The Brazilians flew home on July 14. They were

received quietly in the capital city of Brasilia. As they walked off the plane onto a red carpet, a single government minister shook their hands.

Meanwhile, the country's sports reporters were full of questions and rumors. The Brazilian squad had been ordered not to explain the mysterious events around the final, but this only inflamed people's imaginations. One rumor said that the team had been bribed to lose the final. Another claimed that Ronaldo or even the entire team had been poisoned. Brazilians could not talk about anything else.

The truth was that Ronaldo had been taking medicine to combat his knee problem. He received anti-inflammatories—drugs designed to treat swelling—called Voltaren and Cataflam. He also took several anesthetics, drugs which deaden the nerves in a particular area. This indicated that he must have been injected with the Cataflam and Voltaren, for anesthetics are given to block the pain of a needle. The anesthetics he took had several possible side effects, one of which was seizures.

To make matters worse, it appears his team doctors had been careless with the doses he received—they were desperate to keep him in the lineup. When you combined his stress levels with his drug intake, Ronaldo's strange behavior during the tournament made sense. So did his convulsion.

While his drug-taking was not illegal, it was

revealing. It showed once more just how much pressure professional athletes face. Ronaldo's team was prepared to do anything to keep him on the field. No one stopped to think if he was being harmed by the medication. He simply had to play.

In the World Cup, Ronaldo lost control of his life. He was responding only to others' expectations and needs, not his own. But his career had been that way since the start. His father, uneducated in legal matters, had signed an extraordinary contract with Pitta and Martins. The agents had the right to use Ronaldo's name and image in any way they desired. He had to ask their approval before he signed any other contracts. Even if he signed a business deal without their help, he still had to pay them 10% of the earnings from it.

There was little Ronaldo could do about the situation. If he wanted to end his contract with the two agents, he would have to pay them many millions as a penalty. He was, in reality, their servant. When they told him he had to leave Barcelona for Milan, he had no choice. If they wanted him to go to another team, he would follow orders once more.

Brazilian journalists could not learn the truth behind Ronaldo's World Cup collapse, so they followed him everywhere once he returned to Rio. He would jump into his Mercedes and race away from them, often driving through red lights and risking death. He would change his car several times a day, trying to confuse them. Once, he ripped off his licence plate. Unable to take the attention one day, he screamed: "When will you ever rest? I can't stand this any more."

Ronaldo's countrymen—and the world—often felt sad for him. He had become a tragic figure, a victim. They looked at him and saw a frightened boy swallowed by fame. The image of the perfect superstar, standing on a height greater than they could reach, had crumbled. Yet, in failure, he was almost as likeable as he had been in victory, maybe even more. Now they could relate to him. He was human like them.

In Italy, Ronaldo remained as popular as ever. In November 1998, the small Italian village of Peschici leaped from obscurity into the world news thanks to him. Ninety-nine residents had bought a winning lottery ticket, and they were suddenly $37 million richer.

The women simply wanted to divide the money equally, but their husbands had a plan: to buy Ronaldo from Inter, bring him to Peschici and insert him into their village squad. Their grand idea was dismissed by Inter, who replied that their striker was not for sale. Incidents like this reveal that Ronaldo is not just the greatest soccer player of his era. He is one of the very, very few who rise above defeat and victory: No matter what he does, he is loved and admired the most.

After enduring the Rio media for a while, the striker disappeared for a month in late summer, going to

Mexico and the U.S.A. with Suzanna. As the 1998–99 soccer season began, he rejoined Inter but rarely played. His knee, so ravaged by the World Cup, was healing slowly, and his other knee was inflamed now as well. No one knew when his body and mind would return to normal.

Fate had crowned Ronaldo king of the soccer world in a few short years. He had become a millionaire, as the witch doctor predicted two decades earlier. Now, fate had turned harshly against him, tumbling him off his throne after only four weeks of a French summer. Zinedine Zidane had been the World Cup hero, not him. To complete the reversal, Zidane was named FIFA's World Player of the Year for 1998. Ronaldo finished second in the voting, but he was far behind.

At 22, Ronaldo did not have to worry about losing his skills. Ideally, he could expect another 10 to 12 years of excellence. But the questions remained: Would he be strong enough to recover from the World Cup? Would it make him into a better person and player, or would it destroy him?

He has risen to the challenge before, and he knows he can do it again. Still, if fate has turned against him permanently, Ronaldo faces a greater opponent than any he has met on the soccer field.

Glossary of Soccer Terms

Corner kick: When a defending team is the last to touch the ball before it rolls over its own goal line, a corner kick is taken if no goal has been scored. The attacking team kicks the ball in from the corner of the field closest to where the play ended.

Cross: a pass sent from either the left or right side of the field towards an attacking teammate in front of the net.

Free kick: After a team has committed a foul, the opposing team is awarded a free kick in the place where the foul occurred. The defenders must move back 10 yards.

Fullback: The last line of defense before the goalie.

Header: When a player hits the ball with his forehead, it is called a header.

Midfielder: The middle line of a team which plays either defense or offense.

Penalty box/area: The area immediately around the net measuring 18 yards deep by 44 yards wide.

Penalty shot: If a foul is committed in the penalty area, the attacking team receives a penalty shot. The ball is placed on the 12-yard spot. All defenders must leave the area. One attacker takes a single shot at the goalie, who cannot move until the ball is struck.

Striker: The first line of attack. Teams normally use one or two strikers.

Research Sources

Archer, Michael, Peter Arnold, Christopher Davis, Paul Gardner and Martin Tyler. *The International Book of Soccer.* New York: A & W Publishers, 1977.

Clarkson, Wensley. *Ronaldo! 21 Years of Genius and 90 Minutes that Shook the World.* London: Blake Publishing, 1998.

Kowet, Don. *Pele.* New York: Atheneum, 1976.

Lever, Janet. *Soccer Madness: Brazil's Passion for the World's Most Popular Sport.* Chicago: University of Chicago Press, 1983.

Marcus, Joe. *The Complete World of Soccer.* Pasadena, CA: Ward Ritchie Press, 1977.

Murray, Bill. *The World's Game: A History of Soccer.* Urbana, IL: University of Illinois Press, 1996.

Pele, and Robert L. Fish. *My Life and the Beautiful Game.* Garden City, NY: Doubleday, 1977.

Look for these other

CHAMPION SPORT

BIOGRAPHIES

Tennis

- Martina Hingis
- Pete Sampras

Soccer

- Maradona

Formula One Racing

- Michael Schumacher
- Jacques Villeneuve

Basketball

- Michael Jordan
- Shaquille O'Neal

Boxing

- Muhammad Ali

Figure Skating

- Tara Lipinski